YOUR PLACE
IN THE
COUNSELING
REVOLUTION

YOUR PLACE IN THE COUNSELING REVOLUTION

JAY E. ADAMS

BAKER BOOK HOUSE
Grand Rapids, Michigan

ISBN: 0-8010-0100-5

PHOTOLITHOPRINTED BY CUSHING - MALLOY, INC.
ANN ARBOR, MICHIGAN, UNITED STATES OF AMERICA
1975

CONTENTS

FOREWORD

Because I was deeply concerned about the matters included in this book, I chose the subject for my Staley lectureship of January, 1975 which I delivered to the student body of Cedarville College, Cedarville, Ohio. And because the subject matter is pertinent to those who belong to a larger audience, I am sending these lectures forth to the Christian public in general, hoping that in some measure God will use this humble effort as one small contribution to bringing about the revolution in counseling that may in time spark a new revival of the Christian faith in this country.

The book has been released with two sorts of target audiences in mind. First, this includes the large number of Christian men considering a ministry of Christian counseling. Secondly, I have in mind the average church member who must determine to support efforts made in this direction, or the coming revolution in counseling will not materialize. I want to convince the former that they should consider the work of the pastoral ministry, and I wish to inform the latter about what is happening in the Church of Christ, and enlist not only their support but their participation as well.

If at first the word revolution sounds too sweeping and belligerent, let me urge you to reserve your judgment about this until you have finished reading. By then, I hope that you will see the necessity for nothing less. I like the definition of a revolt (or revolution, as we now call it) in Crabb's English synonyms. He writes:

Revolt. . . signifies originally a warring or turning against the power to which one has been subject; but *revolt* is mostly taken either in an indifferent or a good sense for resisting a foreign dominion which has been imposed by force of arms.

That definition in every way is appropos of the situation that until recently has prevailed. If "force of arms" may be considered figuratively referring to the warnings by which pastors and Christians have been intimidated, the picture is complete. A power, foreign to the Christian Church, has held her tightly in its grips for a long while. There have been many collaborators. But, at long last, tired of the failure, convinced that within the Church itself there are resources that have been virtually untapped, many are awakening to the need and to the opportunities and are beginning to throw off the yoke of oppression. The collaborators, understandably, are not happy. Hopefully, some of them can be won to the cause. But largely, the revolution—as indeed most revolutions are—has begun as a grass-roots struggle. To better alert and inform those at the grass-roots level who sense its importance, I send forth this book. I have revised very little, and have purposely attempted to retain the lecture style. If it seems somewhat abrupt at points, read the text aloud.[1]

---

[1]Tapes of the lectures are available from Westminster Theological Seminary, Chestnut Hill, Pa., 19118.

I.

DON'T BE SHORT CHANGED

I

DON'T BE SHORT CHANGED[1]

Introduction: I thought at first of entitling this address "Anyone who goes to a psychiatrist ought to have his head examined," but thought better of it and settled for "Don't Be Short Changed."

Counselees, or those who urge them to receive counseling, are interested in change. In one way or another, the uppermost concern is to change their lives.

—Perhaps they have *had it* with wives/husbands/parents/children. . . . They want a change.

—Possibly they seek relief from depression or worry or fear or mysterious voices speaking out of nowhere.

—Or. . . they are anxious to learn how to get along with others/how to control tempers/how to communicate with persons they love/how to keep a job/how to rope and tie a runaway sex drive. Any one of these. . . or dozens of other problems. . . impel people everywhere to seek counsel of others, hoping they will provide the change that will bring peace and joy.

Counselors are people who try to help them effect that change. Many of these people who counsel are well meaning and enter the field from altruistic motives; others are themselves confused, seeking answers; some are in the work for the prestige, the power or the money, and some for the gratification of baser desires.

But in this attempt to effect change, profound and

---

[1]Lecture No. 1 was published in a slightly different form in Jay Adams, *Shepherding God's Flock,* Vol. II (Presbyterian and Reformed Publishing Co., Nutley, N. J.), but was delivered as part of the Staley lectureship.

urgent questions arise, such as: Who sets the standard for change? The counselee? The counselor? Someone else? Does the counselee know enough? May the counselor's values be accepted? And—who answers the question about who sets the standard? Who effects the change? Counselee? Counselor? Both? Another? What means will be used for bringing about the change? All those that work? Then is brainwashing acceptable? Surely, there must be *some* limitations in *some* directions—but that's just the problem: where shall the lines be drawn?—and who shall draw them? These and many other similar questions inevitably arise in the minds of all thoughtful counselors.

The trouble is—there isn't one in a thousand who can begin to answer them. Yet, without answers, where are we; what shall counselors do; and what of the counselee?

Counselors read, experiment, debate, write, yet they are no nearer to agreement on these questions than when they first began. Seated in his plush, expensive study, lined with learned tomes, the typical counselor, seemingly serene and secure, is nothing of the sort if he is a man of integrity and a diligent student of his profession. Daily he is harassed by the silent but strong protests over every action he takes and every word that he speaks coming from the authors who observe him from their perches on his shelves. "Too directive," cry some. "Why don't you reflect his feelings?" shout others. "Get rid of all that nonsense about value; focus on the behavior," demands a third. From all sides competing 'isms and 'erapies woo and warn.

In his better moments he tells himself: "Toss the whole business overboard. After all, who can know what is right? I don't even have time to learn all of the systems, with their presuppositions, principles and practices, let alone try them out! Why, there are classical Freudians,

Dynamic Freudians, and Neo-Freudians, Adlerians and Jungians, Logotherapists, Integrity Therapists, Reality Therapists, Radical Therapists, Rational-emotive Therapists, Gestalt Therapists, Contract Therapists, Primal Screamers, Laingians, Transactional Analysts, Skinnerians, Behaviorists by the buckets, Rogerians, Group Therapists, Family Therapists, etc., etc., etc. Why in the world should I suppose that what I am doing is right?"

And. . . think of the poor counselee:—in confusion meandering from one counselor to another—looking for someone who can help him. In the process he is diagnosed, misdiagnosed and rediagnosed. He may be told that he is sick, or that he has been poorly socialized by parents and peers, or that he has been wrongly conditioned, or that his difficulty is genetic, or that he has failed to live up to his full potential. He may be assured that the problem is illness, or bad training or learned behavior, or emotional immaturity, or chemical, or interpersonal or constitutional or existential or whatever in origin. Appropriately he will be treated or trained or encouraged or taught or medicated in widely varying ways. "Let it all hang out," says one. "You need to get it all together," says the next. "Tell me about your childhood, your sex life and your dreams," says another. "Take these pills four times a day and see me in six weeks," or "Renegotiate all of your personal contracts," or "Get rid of those inhibitions—find a man with whom you can have successful sexual relations," or "You must have a series of E.S.T. treatments (i.e., electroshock therapy—or, to put it more realistically, grand mal seizures, artificially induced)," or "We shall recondition your behavior," or "Hypnotism will help," or "Get a frontal lobotomy," or "Talk it out," or "Scream,". . . or. . . . Well, that's just about what one feels like doing when he hears even so small a portion of the whole as this.

In the process, persons have been advised to urinate upon their father's graves, punch pillows until the feathers fly, file for a divorce if they don't get along with a life partner, and just about anything else one could imagine. Before he is through, a counselee may run the gamut, being assured that all will be well if only he medicates, or copulates, or urinates, or meditates or ventilates!

What is he to *do*? In whom shall he *believe*? Where is he to *turn*?

And. . . in the face of all of this uncertainty, don't fail to notice what it is all about. Remember, all of these views, all of these persons, all of these methods are concerned about *changing people's lives*! If physicians were so divided and uncertain, would we entrust our bodies to them? If airlines and airline pilots differed so widely about flying principles and practices, who would fly? Yet, think, people by the millions turn to such counselors to *change their LIVES*! That means—to change their values; to change their attitudes, to change their beliefs, to change their behavior and to change their relationships to significant persons! DARE we allow anyone to meddle in such matters when all is in flux?

Think about the trick a psychiatrist played upon his fellow practitioners—he sent twelve persons— sane as you or I—into twelve of the nation's leading mental institutions for the expressed purpose of discovering how accurate psychotherapeutic diagnosis is. What do you think happened? You guessed it; some of them were wrongly diagnosed as having serious mental illness. How many do you think? Would you believe half? Wrong. Would you believe three-fourths? Still wrong. Would you believe all twelve? Right! *All Twelve*! A one hundred per cent failure!! And, listen to this, of the twelve diagnoses, eleven were diagnoses of schizophrenia! Moreover, these "patients" made no attempt to deceive, but acted normally during the entire period of diagnostic evaluation! No wonder Karl Menninger, commenting on the farce, said: "Schizophrenia is just a nice Greek word."

Surely, by now we should be asking not only where can counselees find help, but also—how can they be protected in their gullibility and vulnerability from misguided (even though well-intentioned), from incompetent, from foolish and from unscrupulous persons? Who (or what) will preserve them from making changes of thought and action that can only disappoint and that may lead to ill consequences equally as bad or worse than those previously experienced?

And, surely, all of this confusion, contradiction and chaos not only must give us pause before approaching or sending someone to the self-styled experts or professionals, it should make us ask an even more basic question: What is behind the disorder or (as Zillborg called it) the "disarray?" Other fields, while having healthy disagreements, seem to make progress and seem to be able to tack down many areas of common agreement. Yet, in counseling, there is a consensus about nothing. Is there not something radically wrong in the discipline of counseling? *What could it be?*

As I gather it, coming here today necessitates an answer to that question. As you might suppose from what I have said, giving that answer is no small task. Indeed, after hearing something of the various opinions and ideologies to which I have alluded, you may wonder why I came— how I could accept the invitation in good faith, and what brings me here anyway. Certainly I could not be arrogant enough to imagine that I had the final word, could I? Do I come to make another vain thrust and thus stir up more sediment to further foul the pool? Dare I even think that I could introduce the idea that would clarify the situation and point toward a pathway that emerges from the fog?

No, if I came with another such word I should be not only a fool but a charlatan. I do not so come.

"Then, what brings you here?" you ask. Answer:

> To point to the path leading to the clear light and sunshine; to explain what is behind the confusion and how it may be swept aside; to herald a new day of counseling that has already begun to dawn—and about which you may possibly hear much more in the not-too-distant future; to challenge you to join the ranks, and to hope that this meagre effort may bear some fruit toward these ends!

"Wait a minute," you reply.

> First, you said that you were not bringing in another opinion or ideology; yet now you seem to say just the opposite. You'd better explain—and make it plain; I've heard just about all I want to take of confusion and contradiction for one day!

> OK; OK—I'll give it to you straight. I have not come to offer one more opinion, system or ideology. I would not dare; as a matter of fact, I wonder continually at the audacity of those who do. Instead, I have come with good news. There is hope in the midst of the chaos; but it is not found in *my way*.

Remember the question I asked earlier, but did not answer? It went something like this: since other disciplines (engineering, business, medicine and even non-clinical and non-counseling psychology) seem to be able to arrive at some measure of order and cohesion—enough at least to produce some concrete results, must not something be radically wrong with counseling? The answer to that question is "yes." Something *is* radically wrong with counseling, and *this is it*: almost to a man counselors have rejected the only true standard of human values, beliefs,

16

attitudes and behavior. Yet those matters comprise the stuff of which counseling is made. They have *looked* everywhere else, *tried* everything else, but have totally *ignored* the one Book that can bring order out of chaos. Only a word from God Himself can properly tell us how to change. In the Bible alone can be found the true description of man, his plight and God's solution in Christ. Only the Scriptures can tell us what kind of persons we must become. Only God can command, direct, and give power to effect the proper changes that will enable men He redeems to renew the image corrupted by the fall. Two Skinnerians in a room with their latest sausage grinder, by which they claim to be able to grind any sort of sausage one wishes, cannot agree about what kind of sausage they want; i.e., what sort of man to produce. Each wants sausage that thinks like himself. God has not only *told* us what man must become, but has *shown* us in Christ! In short, counselors are in their present state of confusion, swayed by every new fad, precisely because they have rejected the one and only perfect and lasting textbook on counseling.

"*Textbook* did you say? The Bible a *textbook* for counseling?" Yes, the Bible is God's basic text for living. It contains "all things pertaining to life and godliness" (II Peter 1:3). In it is all that a counselor or counselee needs to know in order to honor God by loving Him with all that he has, and by loving his neighbor as himself. As a matter of fact, on those two commandments—and in the scriptural explanations of how to fulfill them—hangs all of the work of counseling.

In counseling—per se—we do not find many persons presenting problems about the troubles they are having with *things*. ("You see Doc, there's this chair that I have been having difficulty with. . ." or "I came here to discuss the state of the carburetor on my Toyota.") When those with organic difficulties have been eliminated by sending such persons to physicians, what is left is that large number of people who are in trouble in one way or another with other *persons*—with God and their neighbors.

"But," I can almost *hear* the objection, "you don't use the Bible as a textbook for engineering or architecture or medicine, do you?" Of course not. "Well, then, why do you use it as a textbook for counseling?" Because, while the Bible was never *intended* to be a textbook about business or engineering, God Himself, in the passages cited, as elsewhere, tells us that it *is* a textbook concerned precisely with the problems encountered in counseling. And from the confusion seen uniquely in that field, it should be evident that just such a text is what is desperately needed.

How extraordinary, indeed, it is for Christians, those who claim to believe in the inerrancy and authority of the Scriptures, and who have been saved through faith in Jesus Christ, whose death for their sins is recorded therein, to doubt the fact that the Bible is the textbook for living—and, of course, for effecting every change in living! How could it be otherwise? God alone can tell man what values to espouse; no one else originated the Ten Commandments! God alone can disclose the chief goal of man, explain the core of his problems and offer the fundamental solutions to them. Indeed, if counselors, apart from the Scriptures, could do so, the Bible—and, to be sure, Christ Himself—would have been given in vain! But counselors *cannot*. That is precisely why we are presently in this thick soup.

Well, then, what is the alternative? "There is hope, you say? Then tell me about it—I shall listen cautiously."

To begin with, God everywhere in the Scriptures commands change: "As obedient children, do not be conformed to former lusts. . . but like the Holy One who called you, be holy yourselves also in all your behavior" (I Peter 1:14,15); "You must walk no longer as the heathen walk" (Ephesians 4:17); "Grow by grace, even by the knowledge of our Lord Jesus Christ" (II Peter 3:18). I could go on and on, but you know already that this is true. What you may not have realized, however, is that every biblical exhortation, every insistence upon change, implies hope. God never demands of His children that which He has not provided for them. We are not only *saved* by grace, but our sanctification (i.e., our continued growth and change from sin toward righteousness) as Christians also is the result of God's grace. As Paul told the Galatians, we did not begin the Christian life by grace. . . only to complete it by our own efforts (Gal. 3:3). No, all is of grace. That means, therefore, that God Himself has provided the instructions and the power to live and grow according to them. The instructions—the goals, values, presuppositions, principles and practices— are found in the Scriptures; the power for Christians to live by them is provided by His Spirit. That is the good news about counseling that I bring today. And everywhere—throughout the country—and even else- where in this world, Christian ministers are awakening to the fact. The same Book that says that God has provided what is needed for counseling says also that it has been provided for the equipping of ministers for the work of changing lives: that the *"man of God"* (a term picked up from the Old Testament and used in the pastoral letters to refer to the pastor/teacher) may be adequate, thoroughly equipped. While every Christian should do counseling, it is to the minister that He has assigned the task as a life work.

No wonder there has been confusion! The wrong persons, using the wrong standards, have tried to do all sorts of wrong things without power.

But what of the Christian "professionals," most of whom espouse an eclectic view ("Some from Freud, some from Rogers, some from Skinner. . . and a little from the Bible")? Hal Brooks once said "If you don't know where you are going , any road will do." *That* is the problem with eclecticism. . . it is good only for those who do not know where they are going. Skinner does not eclectically use Rogerian methodology; nor does Rogers use Skinnerian. Why not? Both see man's problem differently and therefore have different objectives in view. Each is committed to the different methodologies that will take them most surely to those destinations. Christians have an entirely different objective than all the rest—to change men so that they may become like Christ. Only God's road leads to that. It is time for Christians to stop riding on the world's bandwagons; they are headed in the wrong direction! The Bible, and the Bible alone, points the way. Therefore, as in salvation, so too in counseling—no other road will do.

But to be more specific, just what *does* the Bible provide? Let us look a *bit* more closely at II Timothy 3 to see.

In this fundamental passage concerning the Scriptures, it is important first to note that their twofold "*use*" or "*purpose*" is described *in terms of change*:

(1) Salvation: they are able to make one "wise unto salvation;" and

(2) for those who *are* saved, they provide four things:

(a) Teaching—they become the standard for faith and life; they show us all that God requires of us.

(b) Conviction—they show us how we have failed to measure up to those requirements in our lives. The word used is a legal term meaning more than to "rebuke" or "accuse" but speaks of pursuing the case to its end *successfully*. The Scriptures show us our sin; they flatten us in repentance.

(c) Correction—the word means (literally) "to stand up straight again." While it is true that the Bible knocks us down, cuts and bruises, rips up and tears down, it is equally true that this is done only to prepare us for its work of picking us up again and heading us in God's proper direction. The Scriptures also bind up and heal; they plant and build. By God's Spirit, who works in and through them, they not only help us put off sin, but also enable us to put on righteousness.

(d) Finally, they "train us in righteousness." It is not enough to quit the past ways, break old habits and stop sinning. If that is all that occurs, one will find himself soon reverting to past ways. He must not only do so, but learn *as a way of life to* walk in the new ways (Ephesians 4).

And what does all of this amount to? Change. We have just been describing the process of *change*. Change in depth. Change as profound as one could imagine. Eternal change. And it is all found in God's Book, the counselor's textbook on human change, the Bible.

I urge you—consider the facts and make the decision. Perhaps God is calling some of you to such a ministry of vital change. If so, answer in faith. With such powerful resources available why should you or your counselees be *short changed?*

II.

THE PICTURE ON THE WALL

II

THE PICTURE ON YOUR WALL

All right. So we have located the fundamental failure in modern counseling—God and His revealed Word have been omitted from the counseling picture. In discussions among counseling people, including Christians, the names of Mowrer, Glasser, Perls, Harris, Rogers, Skinner, Lazarus, Erickson, are more frequently heard and their views are better known than the names of Paul, Peter, David, Solomon and even Jesus Christ. God, and His viewpoint, for most are not a viable option. *That* is the problem. Now what? How can we rectify that situation?

"Isn't that simple enough to answer?" you may ask. "After all, if God is missing from the picture, what we need to do is to bring Him into it."

Well, that reply can be either right or wrong, depending entirely upon what you mean by "bringing God into the picture." The suggestion, of course, is not revolutionary or new. For years people have been writing books with titles like *Psychiatry and The Church, Freud and Christ,* etc. But when you begin to explore the ways and means that have been used to achieve this end, and even how some Christians have conceived of that end itself, you soon begin to recognize that there are problems connected with "bringing God into the counseling picture." The matter is more complex than at first it might seem. And, in my opinion, that is precisely why so many Christians have unwittingly fallen into the sin of accommodationism, which consists of accommodating Christianity to some other view. I find it necessary to define this sin because, it seems, so few say anything about it. Moreover, there is more than one way in which Christian counselors have attempted to include God in their counseling, and as a result, more than one way that accommodationism can take place. And, finally, I think that further study of the problem will convince you that these attempts to bring God into the picture mainly have been unsuccessful.

But, before we turn to the discussion itself let me go one step further and state categorically that this issue is not merely an academic matter. It is not something that we can leave to the counselors to squabble over as an intradepartmental feud. Instead, it is nothing less than a question fraught with large practical consequences for both the counselor and those whom he counsels. The wrong answer to the question involves grave dangers to both, and grave dangers to the Christian Church. Counselor and counselee—alike—stand in personal jeopardy.

"*That* is *strong* language. Are you sure that you are not overstating the hazard? Why do you make such an extreme statement? Wouldn't it be better merely to say that the matter is of *some* moment to all of us because it has practical consequences?"

No, I am *not* overstating the case. Indeed, I will go so far as to say that if God is not brought into the picture properly—i.e., if He is not included in counseling in a manner that accords with what He Himself has required in the Scriptures, it is worse to introduce Him than to leave Him out altogether.

"*Wait* a minute. How can you *say* that? How could leaving God out of the counseling room be less dangerous than including Him—wrongly perhaps—but including Him? Aren't you the one who is always complaining about people leaving God out of counseling? I don't think that I *understand* you. Have I caught you in an inconsistency, or can you clarify what you are saying? I should think that even a little consideration for the place of God in counseling is to be preferred to none."

Well, your question is fair enough, and it surely represents the thinking of many persons today—perhaps some of whom may have influenced you by their writings. But, I must stand by what I have said. And, by the way let me make it clear to begin with, that I do *not* wish to reproach anyone for his good intentions; that clearly is not the issue. There is nothing personal involved in my disagreement with the persons who have attempted to bring God into the counseling picture in ways that I deplore. I can only *commend* every *genuine desire* to introduce God into the counseling context. So there is no inconsistency in what I am saying. The real issue is whether, indeed, the wrong way of bringing God into the picture (to which I have alluded) does anything of the sort. That is to say, the issue is whether He will allow Himself to be brought into the picture that way. And. . . there is *one* personal matter, I confess, that I cannot avoid: *God is a Person*—who does make this sort of thing more than an academic issue with reference to Himself— He takes it personally!

In this brief consideration of the matter, I want you to understand that I can do no more than scratch the surface of the problem; its implications are numerous. I certainly would not claim even to know how many there are. But as I peel off a few bits here and there, I think that you shall see plainly enough from those samples, the depths of the subject that we have chosen to discuss. I shall focus on only one or two of these implications then, and through them try to give you at least some inkling of what I am talking about.

First, one way to bring God into the counseling picture

wrongly is to introduce Him as an *additive*. This adjunctive use of God and His Name dishonors Him as God, denies His sovereignty, and deceives and discourages counselees.

"Wow! That's quite a charge. Can you substantiate it?"

Without a doubt. Ask yourself this question: When God is *added* to an already existing picture, to *what* (precisely) is He added? Well, the very fact that He is needed as an addition tells you, doesn't it?

"What do you mean?"

Just this. If there was a need to bring God into a picture in which He had no place before, the fact is that the picture to which He is added is an *ungodly* one. But I think that you can see that the very idea of associating God with such a picture by attaching God's name to a godless system is repugnant. To attempt to put Him into a system that was designed with no thought of Him, and in the final analysis is (therefore) bent upon leaving Him out is to dishonor Him. God refuses to be thus associated. He will not be identified with the golden calf. He rejects every idolatrous system created by men. Indeed, He declares: "I will not give my glory to another" (Isaiah 42:8). Do you think then that He will allow you to add His Name and that He will give His blessing to any system that was conceived in a proud autonomous spirit, a system, that by its structure finds no need for the living God?

"Well. . ."

There are no wells about it. God will not allow us to add Him on to a system that by its basic presuppositions, by its principles, and by its practices, excludes Him. The result would lead to God's participation in that unequal yoke that He Himself condemns. Christ simply does not associate with Belial!

Therefore, to baptize counseling systems like Freudian Psychoanalysis, Skinnerian Behaviorism, the Rogerian

Human Potential Movement or the Berne/Harris/Steiner views of Transactional analysis into the Christian fold unconverted, by adding on God's holy Name and sprinkling in a few assorted scriptural proof texts, ultimately amounts to taking His Name in vain. It means to represent God as though He were in favor of ungodliness. To say the very least, the attempt to bring God into a picture in which there is no place for Him and into which He will not come can only be futile.

"Well, I can see your point, but are you talking about what people actually do or are you fighting a straw man that wears clothes that *you* bought for him, then stuffed yourself?"

I can assure you that this is no straw man that I have been describing. As I have shown in my books, he is alive and all too healthy; and his practice is widespread. But before I give you a concrete example of what I am talking about, let me at least mention one other implication of the God-as-additive approach.

While the most serious error has been mentioned—i.e., misrepresenting God by saying that He is in favor of godless systems—there is another aspect of that fact: counselees thereby are seriously deceived. By labeling a system Christian, when in fact it has no place for God, the counselor leads his counselees to believe that they are receiving *Christian* counseling (that is to say, counseling that from the ground up is from God; straight from His Word). Affixing a smattering of Christian activities or symbols to that system may give it a Christian appearance, particularly to an uncritical, hurting Christian who is confused and perhaps overly anxious to obtain help. In fact, although the additive counselor himself may be a Christian, and may think and speak of his counseling as Christian, in truth it is not. What is hard for counselees to understand is that the mere fact that a counselor is a

Christian is no assurance that the counsel that he gives is Christian. Yet, the addition of a Christian counselor and Christian trappings to an ungodly system, does not make it more godly. It simply makes it more dangerous. Thereby the true content of the system is disguised. And, as a result, the trusting counselee stands in greater danger because he lets down his guard. If the system were plainly labeled for what it is, he might have been able to protect himself.

"Then that is what you meant when you said that bringing God into the picture wrongly is worse than leaving Him out altogether!"

Exactly. There is no vital change in the picture itself when God words and God symbols are added to it. The picture has been *retitled*. The new title only *misrepresents* the facts; it does not *change* them. The fact that a painting depicts Whistler's mother cannot be altered by renaming her portrait "Whistler's Mother-in-law."

This deception, in which godless systems are depicted as Godly ones has many grave effects upon counselees. Let me mention just two.

On the one hand, this retitling of the picture leads to a false assurance in counselees (and perhaps also in self-deceived counselors). They think that the blessing of God is upon what they are doing when it is likely that it is not. (Of course, it is possible for God to work sovereignly even in such a context if He so wills. But then He will work against the system, in spite of it, and not because of it.) The deception leads counselees to trust in an unscriptural system as if it were biblical, thus according to it an authority and giving to it a kind of submission, that it does not deserve. The presence of a counselor, whose personal Christianity cannot be doubted, the use of prayer and the sprinkling of a sufficient number of Bible verses often is all that it takes to make the deception complete. But these Christian additives, no matter how good they are in and of themselves, will not sanctify systems that (at their core) are godless, and therefore, anti-christian. To put it another way, even when employed by Christians, together with Christian additives, the effect of any anti-christian system always must be harmful rather than helpful. And because God may choose to bless in spite of the sinful circumstances, that does not justify those circumstances for either the Christian counselor or counselee. Nor may either *expect* such help from God in that situation.

And, not only is there a false assurance, but on the other hand, when the system at length fails to produce godly living (and that is something that no ungodly system *can* produce; the fruit of the Spirit grows and is harvested nowhere but in His field), the failure contributes to doubt and despair about God ("God's counsel didn't work," says the counselee).

O.K., I've tried to tell you what it is like to attempt to *add* God to counseling and I appreciate the fact that you have been waiting patiently for my answer to your earlier question. You've been wondering whether anyone really does such a thing or whether I'm beating a stuffed mule. Well, you realize, of course, that people don't *speak* about *adding God* to ungodly systems as I have, but they *do* it. The most recent example of this that I can cite appeared in a widely circulated Christian magazine. In an article on counseling, surveying what Christians are doing today, Vernon Grounds quotes Quentin Hyder as saying,

> The actual psychotherapy I had given him was not significantly different from that which he would have gotten from a non-christian psychiatrist. However, there were three factors which were different. First, he felt more easily able to express his problems in

31

biblical terms and knew that I understood what he was trying to say. Second, being reassured that I was myself a committed believer, he was much more readily able to accept my explanations and respond to my suggestions. Third, I was able to read a few relevant passages of Scripture to him and we often concluded our sessions with prayer together.[1]

Significantly, Grounds comments: "It is this stance and spirit that most Christian counselors appear to identify with today."[2] Notice several things about Hyder's description of his counseling. First, he considers neither the Scriptures nor prayer to be part of the psychotherapy as such. Secondly notice what Hyder added to the pagan system of psychiatry that he uses: biblical terms, a few passages of Scripture and occasional use of prayer. But thirdly, and probably of most importance, notice how the counselee let down his guard. Hyder says that because he was assured that the counselor was a Christian, he more readily accepted the non-christian explanations and suggestions that were offered. The great danger of such a misrepresentation of the facts is that the willing counselee gullibly will accept as Christian what is not because of its Christian packaging.

Just let me mention another example. John Drakeford, Director of the Marriage and Counseling Center at S. W. Baptist Theological Seminary in Fort Worth, Texas, has identified himself so closely with O. Hobart Mowrer that, in fact, the main dish on his menu is little more than Mowrer warmed over. Recently, Mowrer wrote this concerning Drakeford: ". . . when he returned to his

---

[1] *Eternity* Magazine, January 1975, p. 19.
[2] *Ibid.*

seminary he reorganized his whole program along Integrity Group lines." Integrity Groups is the name that Mowrer uses for his humanistic group counseling system. He mentions also a booklet that "Drakeford compiled . . . called 'The Little Red Booklet,' which" (says Mowrer) "is an encapsulated version of Integrity Groups."[3] This booklet is a perfect example of the additive syndrome. After setting forth unadulterated Mowrerian dogma from start to finish, pagan and humanistic as it is, on the last page Drakeford *added* eight Scripture passages! Mowrer does not believe in the existence of God (he told me personally that the Bible could be improved by eliminating the vertical element in it) and his system is from start to finish ungodly; yet Drakeford baptized it unaltered into the faith.

So, you see, I am not tilting at windmills. The problem of using God as an additive to sweeten all sorts of bitter psychiatric potions is a very real one.

Closely related to the additive view (and sometimes linked with it) is what I call the Eureka view. This way of trying to introduce God into the counseling picture differs slightly, but significantly, from the first. This difference makes it all the more subtle and, therefore, all the more dangerous. The advocates of the Eureka view differ from those who follow the first because instead of attempting to bring God in from the outside in order to tack Him on as an adjunct to a godless system, they purport to discover that He was in the picture all the time. The zeal and growing ability of some of these advocates of the view to find all sorts of parallels and similarities as well as outright identifications of Christian truth with pagan theory at times is truly remarkable. As they comb the writings of the framers of the unbelieving systems they

---

[3]Unpublished mimeographed ms., 1974.

may be heard to cry continually, Eureka! as they supposedly discover one after another. Some maintain that there is a positive identification while others, or even the originator of the system, think otherwise. Accordingly, Freud's Id has been identified with the biblical view of original sin, Rogerian listening with the Christian concept of listening, Glasser's idea of responsibility with biblical responsibility and even Skinnerian reward and aversive control with the scriptural reward/punishment dynamic.

In actuality, there is no discovery of anything that was there in the picture; instead, the desire is the father of the fact—God is first projected into the picture, then found. This is accomplished by reinterpreting the contents of the picture to conform to Christian vocabulary. Tragically, at the end one is left with the same picture, but the Bible has been bent to fit it.

"I'm not about to ask you whether you can cite any examples of this trend because I suppose that you can. But tell me this—how can they get away with it? Can't people see that this is going on?"

Well, I'll give you some examples later anyway, but first let me answer the immediate question that you have raised. Remember from the previous discussion how gullible and disarmed a Christian can be when he is anxious to get relief from a pressing problem and he finds a Christian "professional" who claims to be using Christian counseling. Add to that the psychotherapeutic jargon and the ethos that the medical model lends to the *psychiatrist*, and you have the basic ingredients for easy acceptance. The poor counselee may think, "I don't see it," but then he remembers that Dr. so-and-so says that it is so, and he acquiesces. "After all," he reasons, "the good Dr. said that the problem was too deep for me anyway." Moreover, many things that unbelievers suggest do resemble Christian methodology. But careful investigation of similarities always reveals fundamental differences.

The problem of the Eureka mentality is a serious one; the practice of crying Eureka is nearly universal. In an almost ludicrous statement, Marion Nelson wrote: "I have never found any command or exhortation in the Bible which, properly translated, interpreted and applied, contradicts any psychological principle." I say that this is almost ludicrous, because at first it brings a chuckle as one thinks of Nelson trying to retranslate and reinterpret hundreds of Biblical passages in order to square them with thousands of conflicting psychological principles made by the advocates of scores of conflicting systems. But upon further reflection the smile must give way, for it is because of the acceptance of this palpable nonsense that many lives will be ruined. The only way for Nelson to support his thesis, so far as I can see, is for him to judge which principles are the true psychological principles. He could only do this, of course by using a standard, and if that standard is the Bible, then the statement is nonsense since the Bible would eliminate all principles which conflicted with it.

Gary Collins is perhaps typical of the tendency to cry Eureka. In his book,[4] *Effective Counseling,* he not only equates Fromm's view of love with I Corinthians 13, but even finds Freud in favor of religion.[5] Without saying more, let me finally mention the astounding statement of L. I. Granberg, who had the temerity to write: "The Christian who considers thoughtfully the findings of the psychotherapist sees many of the processes associated with the Christian's rebirth and sanctification operating

---

[4]Marion Nelson, *Why Christians Crack Up* (Moody Press, Chicago: 1960), p. 16.

[5]Gary Collins, *Effective Counseling* (Creation House, Carol Stream: 1972), p. 59.

in another context and described in a different vocabulary."[6] How blind men can be, to identify what psychiatrists do with that which the Bible teaches may be done by the Holy Spirit *alone*. Paul plainly states, in I Corinthians 2, that the natural man neither understands the Spirit's work, nor what has happened to men who have been transformed by His work.

Usually the pious label that is gummed on the Eureka process is "common grace." But common grace is another thing. It does not mean that pagan dogma can be taught as Christian truth by translating it into Christian terms. The goodness of God is manifested in common grace as He makes the sun to shine upon both believers and unbelievers alike. He restrains evil in unbelieving men so that they do not totally destroy one another, and He allows them to excel in many of the arts and crafts of society. But, as Calvin so well put it, "many monstrous falsehoods intermingle with those minute particles of truth scattered up and down their writings. . . . To the great truths, what God is in Himself, and what He is in relation to us, human reason makes not the least approach."[7] And, as we saw in the previous lecture, it is with those truths that counseling deals.

In short, every Christian must become wary of the sort of confused thinking that leads both counselors and counselees alike to conclude that any slight alteration of the prevelant pictures of counseling will do. No such tinkering with ungodly systems will ever make them Christian. We can settle for nothing of the sort. Nor can we merely hang another picture in their midst. No indeed; all of the pictures must be removed from the wall. In their

---

[6]L. I. Grouberg, "Counseling," Baker's Dictionary of Practical Theology (Baker Book House, Grand Rapids: 1967), p. 194.

[7]John Calvin, *Institutes* III, IV, 4.

place a new one must be hung. It is a picture into which God and His Word are neither intruded as an extraneous appendage, nor is it one in which He is projected and then discovered. Rather, God is in the *background* of the picture at every point, *He* is its theme and its subject, and certainly not of the least importance is the fact that He Himself is the artist who painted it. When we hang that picture on the wall of every Christian counseling room, the world will begin to cry EUREKA—at last we've found it!

III.

TURNING THE TIDE
BY COUNSELING

III

TURNING THE TIDE BY COUNSELING

"We see the problem as you have presented it. You've helped us to understand how some Christians have wrongly tried to solve it. But now, don't you think it's time to say something about what can be done to turn this sad situation around? After all, we are looking toward our futures in the Lord's vineyard. And many of us do not yet know how our gifts ought to be used there. Perhaps you can say something that will be of help."

An extremely reasonable request. And, I am so entirely caught up with it that I plan to spend the time in both today's and tomorrow's lecture talking about it. What I hope to show you today is that counseling is tied far more closely to your future than you may realize.

To begin with, I want you to understand that the opportunities for serving Christ were never greater than they are today. You will take your place in the church and in society at a remarkable time. The decline of the liberal churches, the political and moral confusion on every hand, and the self-confessed failure of psychiatry and psychology to really help men with their problems have combined to make people everywhere examine again the basic issues of life. People everywhere are beginning to recognize the need for what you have. To meet that need, God has been blessing His faithful churches with numbers, finances, resources and increasing influence. The time is ripe for a sweeping proclamation of the saving gospel of Jesus Christ, with its impact for good in every area of our culture. All is ready. All, but *one* thing. . . .

There is one major obstacle: Christians. Christians by

the thousands, just like their non-christian neighbors, are suffering from unresolved personal problems. They are turning in droves to counselors of all sorts. Pastors are overburdened by husbands or wives threatening to dissolve their marriages, by parent/teen struggles, and by interpersonal conflicts among various members of their flocks. There is immense power abroad in the church today, but much, if not *most* of it is being drained off by these energy-wasting difficulties. If even a small proportion of the energy of God's people that is now consumed in anxiety, worry, guilt, tension, anger and resentment were able to be released into productive activity for the kingdom of God, the world would soon know that Jesus Christ is at work today. Sadly, instead, the world still searches for the answer to its problems, seeing little or no difference in the lives of professed Christians.

Yet, potential for untold change now exists; God has enmassed in the church an enormous amount of resources that are virtually untapped. Were the holes in the barrel, through which so much power is being lost, repaired, the effect for good could be overwhelming. In a vital sense, then, a necessary preliminary to any real impact upon those around us who do not know Christ, is for us to become the sort of Christians whose lives, in the midst of confusion and chaos nevertheless, shine. But shining lives today are rare. The church is shot through with the same attitudes toward life that may be found in any other place. There is little distinctive living. Christians look too much like the world. God has told us that usually it is not our distinctive teaching or belief that first makes an impression, but rather, as Peter explained to Christian wives, they would have to win their unsaved husbands without a lot of talk by *demonstrating* their faith in daily living (I Peter 3:1,2ff.). What Peter told wives, holds true elsewhere: when others *see* Christianity in action, they will be ready to *hear* about it in words.

That's where counseling comes in. Not only is there the need for the kind of counseling that always was and always will be essential to the welfare of the church and to the evangelization of those unsaved persons who come to Christians for help, but if I am not entirely mistaken, in this period of national breakdown there is a special need for Christian—truly Christian—counseling. If the church can be repaired, the holes plugged, and the power preserved and harnessed, the effect upon the surrounding society might even occasion another Great Awakening. Surely, the need is apparent. The opportunity appears to be present too. But will we seize it? That is the question that I come here to put to you. All of the evangelism programs that may be conceived, no matter how true and how biblical, will not bring about the desired results if on two fronts weakened lives stand in the way. First, as I have indicated already, Christians must be strengthened in the witness of their lives, demonstrating in their personal decisions, in their practical actions and in their expressed attitudes and comments that Jesus Christ enables them to weather the economic, political and social storms that are raging uncontrolled. Indeed, others need to see in us that peculiar combination of realistic joy and peace that comes from righteous living empowered by the Holy Spirit (cf. Romans 14:17). Secondly, Christians whose lives are weakened by unending strife and turmoil make poor recruits for evangelism. They are too much embroiled in their own problems to be of much help to others. So, in one sense, it does not seem to be going too far to say that today proper counseling is a prerequisite for evangelism.

But be that as it may, how shall we reach the goals that we have described? What sort of strategy must be followed in order to plug so many holes soon: Where will the counselors come from and how shall they be trained? How shall we alert the Church to the solution, and convince Christians that there is hope even in the midst of the present disorder? Those are large questions that require more detailed answers than I could offer here. Yet, they are not abstract issues; they are deeply practical, and you will be involved in their answer, because you belong to the generation that will constitute the emerging leadership that can either carry the day or lose the battle. The outcome largely will depend upon how well you enter into, energize, more sharply define and bring to its fullest flower, the counseling movement that some from our generation have conceived and have gotten under way. We have begun and I hope begun well (that will be for your generation finally to determine). But, at any rate, the real task we must bequeath to you. We stand near the close of a transition period; most of us will die in the wilderness. It is up to you to lead the Church into the promised land.

So, if you are going to take up the challenge, you will need to know something of the history of what has happened so far, as well as what is expected of you in the future. You need perspective. It is hard to know where to begin, but perhaps it would be best to go back to the situation that existed when some of us entered the ministry about twenty five years ago. Liberals were riding high; they had nearly all of the ecclesiastical clout that did not belong to the Roman Catholic Church. Conservative churches were in the minority, weak in finances and nil in national influence. Great blows successively had been struck at the church. Evolution had all but successfully destroyed belief in creation and in the fall of man. Adam had come to be considered but a mythical character. That meant that the whole question of man's sin in Adam and the consequences of the fall were up for grabs. To move from questions about the origins of man and his fall into sin to doubts about the second Adam and His death for guilty sinners was but a short journey. None, however, except the most extreme wanted to eliminate Christ from the picture; after all, His life and many of His words could be used (or misused) to support some of the idealist values and programs of the new humanism. So, through the advent of a so-called higher criticism of the Bible that purported to be *scientific*, Jesus was stripped of His deity and made instead to be the first and best Christian. His role became that of an example and a teacher who taught self-sacrifice and good deeds. By following in His steps we could bring about a new and better world in which to live. The portions of the Scriptures that so obviously taught the miraculous and the redemptive, and that contradicted the views of the liberals, were no problem to them since the Scriptures were no longer considered to be *God's* revelation to man, but *man's* best endeavor (to date) to reveal God. They were conditioned by their times (as indeed, was Jesus Himself), and they were caricatured as filled with local and dated elements. Belief in the Supernatural (to which now "Science" had given the gate) posed no problem, since it could be discarded as a form of magic. After the layers of such accretions had been scraped away, and after the mythology had been reinterpreted in scientific terms, presumably one could find the true historical Jesus and his teaching lurking behind. It was simple enough for each one to remove what was not wanted at any point by this highly subjective process.

Well, the attacks were relentless and the gains were substantial. Everywhere, denominations, institutions of learning and organizations that had been developed by Bible-believing Christians and dedicated to the service of the Lord Jesus Christ fell into the hands of unbelievers.

Funds, resources, programs and institutions which had been given to further the teaching of the gospel now were used to destroy faith. Those few who did not capitulate, those men and women who under trial, loss and even persecution held true to the Word of God, were thrown on the defensive. Energies that previously could be used for the positive work of evangelism and edification were now spent in fighting battles, most of which took place within the borders of the church itself. Many of these battles were lost. For the badly outnumbered, battle-worn troops, that meant retrenching. With supplies, personnel, resources and strategic positions all in the enemies hands, they found themselves faced with the mammoth task of rebuilding again what had crumbled, but this time not in virgin territory; it had to be done in the midst of the Samaritans who did all that they could to hinder. Vast amounts of energy were consumed in these battles and in the rebuilding of the church in America. The critics jeered, the opposition sneered, and even capitulating Christians (of which the woods was full) heaped discouragement upon the faithful few who from their several denominational and ecclesiastical backgrounds tried once more to build on a sure foundation. The in-fighting had been exhausting; the opposition had been bold and ruthless; but the current situation shows plainly enough that in spite of all, God has blessed those who persevered.

But there were losses even in the ultimate gains. With energy consumed in waging war within and without, with resources and manpower poured into rebuilding, there was little energy and little time left over to spend cultivating one's personal and family faith. Few books, few efforts were forthcoming in these areas. Consequently, the Church, the family and the individual suffered greatly. Some Christians, indeed, forsook the battles and the rebuilding and went off to the caves. There they developed subjective mystical and deeper life concepts based upon individual communion with God and personal experience. But far from helping the situation, this factor brought more division and confusion. Then too, there were those who saw in the defeats and the growing apostasy, the end at hand and, in the spirit of eleventh hour thinking, gave up all hope of restoring the faith. Their energies also were diverted and dissipated as they turned to the study of prophecy with *such* a vengeance that little else mattered.

In all this, concerns about Christian living were largely missing. In the confusion, church discipline evaporated. Personal ministry of Christian to Christian was mostly unknown. Young people were raised with little or no instruction about marriage or the home. They were taught the doctrine that they needed, to withstand the foe—and that was good—but rarely were they taught either the implications of biblical truths for daily living or how to study the Bible in such a way that one can discover those implications. My generation therefore has grown up knowing little or nothing about these matters. Consequently, our homes and our lives have suffered. We have made some terrible mistakes. Nor have we taught our children what they needed to know—that is why some of you find yourselves in some of the dilemmas that you face right now. Currently, evidence of that need is apparent in the size of the crowds that seek help from those who give such basic instruction.

Some of us who have begun our Christian lives and have entered into our ministries during this period of tumultuous upheaval, have found ourselves veering from one of these emphases to another. But, as a consequence at last we have come to see the great need for balance. We fought, and were ourselves at times consumed with fighting. We built, and often became so weary in the work that at times we became weary *of* the work. We argued prophetic viewpoints until we were able to divide and subdivide not only the times and the seasons, but ourselves. We lived at church and found no time to live before the world and in our homes. Now we have come full circle. We want to hand you a better and more balanced approach, one, that while neglecting none of these emphases, nevertheless knows how to put each in its proper place according to biblical priorities. That is one reason why I have tried to paste together this historical/ personal collage for you. It would be wrong for me to entreat you to put an emphasis upon counseling which is unquestionably *needed* at present, if by doing so I were to cause you to neglect the other factors that are essential to maintaining the faith collectively and individually. That is also one reason why I have tried to point out what I think is a valid connection between counseling and evangelism. In other words, I am trying to get you to see that a strong emphasis upon counseling is the strategy for today. But at the same time, I want to warn you that if we are to enter into the opportunities that lie just ahead, we must not reject the emphases of the past, imbalanced as they may have been at times, and we must not become so caught up in counseling and biblical truth about Christian living that we forget other vital matters. While the practical must not be sacrificed for the doctrinal, neither is it right to move in the opposite direction. We must not lose the true gains that have been won so dearly by creating a *different*, but nonetheless, *another* unhealthy imbalance.

There is need for continued doctrinal warfare with the forces of the evil one. The building of the church must have our continued efforts. Zeal for Evangelism and missions must not flag. Prophetic study is important. But, while doing these things we must also restore the home and the quality of relationships that we sustain to one another and to God. Otherwise, all of these other efforts will be in vain. Yet, we may not allow this concern to water down our theology like those who have been teaching what is called the new Relational Theology. Those who have taken more than a *taste* of Keith Miller's *New Wine*, have become *intoxicated* with it and have found their ability to walk in the straight paths of biblical orthodoxy, seriously impaired. Theology does not come from experience; it always must issue from the Scriptures. Experience must be judged by the Bible. What we need, then, is not a new theology, but a concern for personal living that grows out of a solid theology and that at every point is conditioned by it.

So, Christian young people, I call you to get involved in the need of the hour. Get involved by beginning to square off your own life with God and with your neighbor. Examine each area of your life to discover how anger and resentment, fear and worry, envy and personal ambition, laziness and lack of discipline, guilt and depression have been hindering the development of your gifts for ministry and service to one another and to the world that so desperately needs to hear of a Savior. Take an inventory of your relationships, beginning with your relationship to God. Are you in proper fellowship with Him and with your parents and peers? You cannot begin to counsel others until you have begun to learn how to receive God's counsel for *your* life.

When you have sufficiently attended to these matters, and when you have learned how to maintain loving relationships with God and your neighbor, get involved in helping others. There are so many who need your help. Some of you will be called to counseling as a life calling in the ministry. Others will not. Nevertheless, you must recognize that God has called every Christian to a ministry of counseling someone at sometime. In a number of passages every Christian is called to become competent to counsel someone.[1] But, in closing, let me just read one other passage to you that says it so clearly:

> Brothers, if a man is caught in any tresspass, you who are spiritual should restore him in a spirit of gentleness, looking to yourself, lest you too be tempted. Bear one another's burdens, and so fulfill the law of Christ (Galatians 6:1-2).

> That is what we need—and by the grace of God that is what we shall have if you respond in obedient faith!

---

[1]Cf. esp. Romans 15:14; Colossians 3:16; these verses strongly attest to the fact.

IV.

YOUR PART IN
THE COUNSELING REVOLUTION

IV

YOUR PART

IN THE COUNSELING REVOLUTION

Today we come to the concluding lecture in this series. It is last, but in many ways it is the most important of all. I could not present what I have to say until first I took time to set the stage for it. That, either adequately or poorly, I have done. Let me summarize what I have said. The current despair and disorder both within and without the church create the need. Combined with that, the growing resources accumulated by the faithful churches of Christ newly emerging as the victors in the century-long struggle with liberalism, provide the opportunity. The roadblock to seizing the opportunity, and thus meeting the need, is the weakness of Christians themselves, and the resultant weakness of a church that, otherwise, might be powerful. An outstanding and strategic answer to this problem, that will plug the holes and conserve energy, that will repair the disunity and bring about the release of the strength of love working in concerted effort, is biblical counseling. But Godly counseling will not be forthcoming, if we incorporate the world's failures into the church baptizing them as Christian when, in fact, they are not; rather, it is only to be attained by digging deeply into the mine of scriptural truth to discover those presuppositions, principles and practices that God so graciously has provided, and that we so ungratefully have neglected. God's power in the church is going to be released widely, with great impact both within and without, only when

Christians everywhere begin to straighten out their lives and their homes before Him and before one another. Then in the spirit of gentleness they may begin to minister both formally and informally to one another. That, as I say, is the background that I have tried to sketch out. Now against that background, let me explore the last statement in some depth. We shall bring it into the foreground. It is this: God has obligated Christians to minister to one another both formally and informally as each other's counselors.

Counseling, as you already know from the quotation with which I ended the last lecture, as well as from other sources, is not unknown in the Bible, nor was it unknown to the Churches of the New Testament. Galatians 6:1,2 is explicit: each individual, as God gave him occasion, was to restore his brother whenever the need for such restoration was necessary. He could not remain disengaged. Whenever, in the providence of God, he discovered a brother caught in any sin from which that brother was unable to extricate himself, he was obligated to move in and help. That, in contrast, is rarely done today. And, it is clear from the large number of passages that have to do with mutual ministry in the New Testament, that this practice was universally taught by the apostles and was followed widely. Many of the scriptural passages that require this sort of activity contain the key words "one another," and many of the "one another" verses refer to exhortation, encouragement, restoration, admonition, rebuke and the giving of other sorts of counsel.[1] What is of greatest importance to note is that all of them are concerned not with the ministry of someone who is called to counseling as a life calling, but with the ministry of individual, every-day-man-in-the-pew Christians to one another.

---

[1] Cf. Galatians 6:2 to begin with.

While it is impossible to provide the training or know-how for counseling that you as a Christian may need in a lecture series like this, it is proper to urge you to consider your responsibility to find such help. Much of what you lack can be obtained by personal study of the subject as it is taught in the Word of God. God will bless you with increasing wisdom and finesse if you prayerfully and earnestly search the Scriptures and faithfully attempt to put into practice what you find there. But remember you must show in it all the spirit of gentleness. The biblical encouragement to engage in counseling of one another is given with that clear qualification. Increasingly, other helps to understanding and applying the Scriptures are becoming available. Books, short courses, counseling materials and courses on cassettes have been prepared for such purposes.[2] Moreover, and of the greatest importance, many pastors who themselves have been studying their obligations anew and who also have become concerned about mobilizing their congregations for mutual ministry, are preaching about these matters and conducting courses to supply what is needed. It may well be that with some slight encouragement on your part your pastor would be willing to organize a course of study in your church.[3] Many pastors as a first step already are working with their elders and deacons to prepare them to join in the work of counseling.

But mutual ministry means more than merely helping others; it also means willingness to ask for and to receive help from others when needed. There is no one of us who at some time or another does not need the counsel of his brother. We must not become too proud or too

---

[2]For a list of publications, see inside back cover.

[3]One way to begin might be to purchase a copy of *Shepherding God's Flock*, Vol. II, as a gift for your pastor. The book discusses the concept of lay counseling. See inside back cover.

embarrased (which is only another way of saying the same thing) to seek help when we recognize that we are at the end of our own resources. What God has provided through brotherly counsel we dare not turn down. It is not always easy to accept help from another. But whenever a brother approaches us to resolve some problem between him and ourselves, or to restore us when he thinks that we are caught in a trespass, we must learn to humble ourselves and receive him with thanksgiving. It helps to remember that in so doing, he is being obedient to God. His effort honors God because he honors God's Word by following it (cf. Matthew 18:15ff.). We must be thankful for that, no matter how difficult anything else in the encounter may seem. And remember too, probably you should have taken the initiative yourself before it had to come this (cf. Matthew 5:23,24). There is none of us who from time to time, would not be all the better off for having had just such an encounter.

Now let us consider the second way that you can further the counseling movement in the days ahead. I can report that there is a significant amount of concern to become involved in biblical counseling abroad in the land today. During the last two years I have been receiving upwards of a hundred or so letters each year from young men (not to speak of young women who write) who are majoring in psychology and who have decided to enter the field of Christian counseling. A fair number even come for personal interviews. Most of them want me to make some recommendation about the proper graduate training to get in order to prepare themselves for a ministry of Christian counseling. I make one reply: "If God has called you to the work of fulltime counseling then go to a good theological seminary. *That* is the proper place to obtain the training that you need. And when you are through, get ordained and serve Christ in a pastorate, because *that* is the proper place in which to do Christian counseling as a life calling.

"Incredible! What do you have in mind when you steer them into the seminary and then into the formal ministry of the Word? Are you interested in luring more students to Westminster?"

No, that is not my goal. As a matter of fact, I consider it just as much my job as a seminary professor to keep the wrong men out of the pastorate as it is to persuade the right ones to enter it. We already have too many men in pastoral ministry who do not belong there. We don't need any more of the sort. What I have in mind is just this: a *number* of those who write are precisely the sort of men who *ought* to consider the gospel ministry seriously. They have exactly the right qualities and the proper concerns, but they have never considered the ministry. Reasons vary, of course, but for many I discover, it is the model of the pastor, and the model of the pastorate they have known that has turned them off. A part of this grows out of the matter of balance of which I spoke in the previous lecture, and the weaknesses of both the members of the congregation and many pastors in the areas of Christian living and personal confrontation. But when I sketch for them something of the biblical picture of a pastor and something of his work as it could be carried on, some begin to reexamine their goals. A number of these men now are preparing to serve Christ in the pastorate.

Now, in order to give you some indication—and of necessity what I say must be greatly abbreviated—of what the pastoral ministry of the future will be like, when carried on by men well-trained in biblical counseling, who intend to do the proper work of the pastor (rather than all sorts of things to which God did not call them), I shall offer a slice of an imaginary, but typical sort of conversation with one of these men.

"The pastorate? Why do you suggest that? All of that visitation, organizational work, and preaching is not for me. I want to work with people and to help them to get out of their problems."

I am certain that you do, but that's exactly why I suggested that you consider the pastorate. You see, there is no better place in which to do what you want to do than in the pastorate. And it is just the very combination of factors that you think would keep you from truly helping people out of their difficulties (organization, preaching and visitation) that God designed to accomplish that purpose. Any other sort of counseling endeavor that you undertook would be severely truncated, in comparison to the work of the pastoral ministry, by the omission of these factors.

"Frankly I don't see it. You are going to have to spell it out a lot more clearly than that before I could buy it."

Gladly. Let's begin by taking up one of your previous comments. You want to help people get out of trouble, is that right?

"Exactly. I can think of few things more rewarding."

Fine, but let me help you consider one that might be. Here you are five or six years from now, deeply involved in the work of counseling. You have just said goodbye to the third person this week who came in with the same problem. Who knows how many times before and after you will see others with that problem. Under your breath you say to yourself as she leaves, "If only I could get on the housetop and warn people before they got themselves into this mess; here is the third case this week!" But, alas, you can't. The counseling that you do is remedial, not preventive. It is repair work, after the fact. But, God designed a place where there is a rooftop from which to issue the warning—the Christian pulpit. There you can warn, rebuke, encourage and guide men, women, and children around those pot holes into which so many have stumbled. Preaching, among other things, is preventive counseling. Organizational work gives you an opportunity to plan for proper teaching in the Church School, Youth Group, etc. You can't do preventive work without access to people early enough to help them avoid the dangers. And nothing can reach them like an organized program. Moreover, before things grow so bad that it is hard to do anything about them, as a pastor you have the opportunity and the right to initiate counseling. Nipping problems in the bud, before they ever get so large that the person might think about consulting a counselor, is a significant part of true pastoral concern (which, incidentally, is what the word visitation means in the Bible). That word does not mean making all sorts of useless house calls, as some have misunderstood it to mean. It means shepherdly concern that leads to whatever help is needed. When the Bible speaks of "visiting widows and orphans," for instance, obviously it does not mean to make house calls on them; it means to look after them, to care for their needs). So, if you are really concerned about helping people get out of difficulty, you certainly should be equally as concerned, if not even more concerned about keeping them out of those difficulties in the first place. And the person who can do this best is someone who has had to help pick up the pieces in remedial counseling. Only the pastorate provides a balanced opportunity to do both preventive *and* remedial counseling.

"O.K., I can buy that, but what about all of the other organizational activities that a pastor has to become involved in?"

Well, the problem is that some pastors have become involved in many things that they have no business doing, and have failed to do the things that they ought to do. I am interested in seeing you consider the ministry because I suspect that you would not be like many of the pastors who have failed in this way. You see, you are not rejecting the pastorate that is described in the New Testament; what you dislike or fear is a model that was originated in modern times. For example, organization, in the New Testament was structured in order to do two things: to allow the pastor become a pastor and teacher (and nothing else) and to allow the entire congregation to exercise their gifts in mutual ministry to one another and to the world around, and to assist the pastor in his work. It is all found in concise form in Ephesians 4:11,12, but it is worked out in detail in many other places. Let me quote those two verses for you:

> God gave some. . . to be pastors and teachers, for the equipping of the saints for their work of ministry.

> That is the New Testament picture. A pastor is a shepherd; the prime task of a shepherd is to know and to care for his sheep. You get the picture when you read the twenty third Psalm this way: "The Lord is my pastor; I shall not lack." It is the shepherd's task to provide the concerned care for sheep that God requires. A large part of that will involve personal counseling (cf. Acts 20:31). Christ, the chief Shepherd, set the pattern for all of His undershepherds, by laying down His life for His sheep.

"I never thought of it that way."

You haven't heard the half of it. The pastor can counsel with authority—the authority of the living God Himself, as he counsels in His Name. He has the power of church discipline. Moreover, he can provide *total* care for the counselee; not merely care that extends to one hour one day a week. He can follow up his counseling as no other counselor is able to. And think of the resources that are available to Him. He has an entire congregation to draw upon. To assist him in counseling, he has their prayers, their strengthening reassimilation of a forgiven offender, and their many specialized abilities, to name but a few. Take the latter. Why should the pastor spend his time as a counselor helping a counselee to get his finances in shape when he has a half dozen men in the congregation who are experts in such matters? At that point in his counseling, he simply makes an appointment with one of them for the counselee and thus provides expert help while reserving his own counseling time for what could not be supplied by others. Moreover, by involving him, he has helped another member to use his gifts in ministry and thus has brought blessing to someone else. If a place is needed for a young person to stay while he is trying to kick a drug habit, he has six homes in his congregation ready and able to provide the needed care. He has trained the members of those homes himself. If. . . .

"Wait a minute, I don't know many churches like *that*!"

I agree, you probably don't. That is one reason why you have not considered the pastorate. But there are *some*, and increasingly we see more; there will be *many* more when young people like yourself catch the vision for the pastorate that is set forth in the Scriptures rather than shying away because they see in most of today's congregations and in many of their pastors something quite foreign to this. I do not say that it will be easy to make all of the changes that are necessary to bring this about. Pastors now working at it have discovered that it can be hard. But it is possible. And by God's grace it can happen all over. The idea must be taught and Christians everywhere must become convicted about the need. The change will require nothing short of a revolution. Even if you are not called to counseling as a life ministry, you can help by supporting such efforts, as indeed a growing number of laymen are today. I did not say that it would be easy. But a man with the heart of concern for people that *you* show is just the sort of man that God loves to use to bring about such things.

And, let me mention one final fact. The place to study for a counseling ministry is in a good theological seminary, because *that* is the only place where an adequate education for counseling as a life calling can be obtained. I am not referring primarily to the counseling courses offered in such institutions. Rather, I am thinking of the Greek, and of the Hebrew, and of the theology, and of the exegesis courses and so forth; those studies that enable one to become intimately and accurately acquainted with the Bible. That is what a counselor needs above all. If he is to withstand the pressures of the age, if he is to rely on the living God and not upon the wisdom of men, if he is to help counselees to love God and to love their neighbors as they should, he must have "the Word of Christ dwelling in him richly" (Col. 3:16). That is the basic need for counselors today.

Well, you have heard me out. I don't know whether you have been influenced by what I have tried to say or not. But one thing I know; you already are involved in counseling more than you may recognize and that involvement will increase. Remember, what you do to support biblical counseling may make a great deal of difference not only to you, and some day to your children, but also to the future course of the church of Jesus Christ in the land. May God convict you all of the great need, and of the great opportunity that lies at hand, and move you to do whatever you should.

BOOKS BY JAY E. ADAMS